The Yenta's Guide to No-Sweat Exercise

Stretch & Kvetch

By Raye Ann Greenbaum & Jackie Tepper
Illustrations by Betsy Hoffman

Stretch and Kvetch:

The Yenta's Guide to No Sweat Exercise

Yenta (Yen'te), *Yiddish*, noun: a busy-body
Kvetch (Kvetch), *Yiddish*, verb: to complain

By Raye Ann Greenbaum
&
Jackie Tepper

© Copyright 2000, Raye Ann Greenbaum and Jackie Tepper

All rights reserved.
No part of this book may be reproduced, stored in a retrieval system, or transmitted by any means, electronic, mechanical, photocopying, recording, or otherwise, without written permission from the author.

ISBN: 1-58820-067-1

To Carolyn, Esther, and Nan whose stretching and kvetching inspired us to write this book

Acknowledgments

We wish to express our deep appreciation to Rick Taylor and Jerry Holthouse whose professional expertise allowed us to stretch more, kvetch less and breathe a whole lot easier.

We would also like to thank Arlene Lebovitz who read the exercises as they were written and offered advice and encouragement.

Contents

Introduction ix

Chapter I
The Mah Jongg Stretch 1

Chapter II
The Worry Walk 11

Chapter III
The Jewelry Lift 19

Chapter IV
The Shopper's Pull 25

Chapter V
The Beach Bends 33

Chapter VI
The Bean and Barley Upper
Arm Reducer 39

Chapter VII
Eavesdropper's Eye Strengthener and Jowl Firmer Isometrics 45

Chapter VIII
The Cellular or Portable Phone Twist 53

Chapter IX
Challah or Pumpernickel Knead 61

Chapter X
Watch the Grandchildren Stairclimber and Complete Workout 65

Chapter XI
When Calories Don't Count and other *Bubameicies 79

Chapter XII
Calorie Count of Favorite Snacks 85

Chapter XIII
A Yenta's Favorite Names and Numbers 91

Chapter XIV
Blank Pages 95

Epilogue 101

Introduction

This book is for anyone fifty or older who wants to be on an exercise program, who *needs* to be on an exercise program, or who has tried exercise programs only to find them boring, strenuous, time consuming, and slow to show results.

You have a closet full of walking shoes, running shoes,

step shoes, and cross trainers; more pairs of tights than Baryshnikov; and your treadmill is gathering dust in the spare bedroom.

Your gym memberships are in the multiples, and after an hour of huffing and puffing with perfectly-chiseled aerobics instructors, you find yourself easing your sorrows (or congratulating yourself on your efforts) by scarfing a pint of

Ben and Jerry's most chocolate, crunchiest fudgiest ice cream.

You're tired of wondering if calories do or don't count, if you should eat more or less protein, and if your daily food groups should include red wine, white wine, or no wine. And you've vowed that if Pritikin, Ornish, Atkins, and Jenny Craig don't work this time, maybe next time you should call Kevorkian.

You're looking for exercise you're not even aware *is* exercise. Well, here's our solution. First, forget the weights and isometrics, forget the "10 weeks to thin thighs and flat tummies," and *please*, forget trying to figure out what body type you are. Throw away the charts that show how many calories you burn by vacuuming and mopping (hopefully you *hire* someone who burns calories that way).

We are not doctors, exercise physiologists, nurses, or nutritionists. We're **yentas.** A yenta is a gabber, a know-it-all, one possessing a busy mind.

And to us, a busy mind makes a "busybody"; hence this guide was created. Yentas can *always* make "something out of nothing," and if this book makes you smile, well, you've successfully endured your first no-sweat exercise.

This book is for *you*. We hope you'll like it. If not, there's always a new class starting next Tuesday....

Chapter I
The Mah Jongg Stretch

(The yenta's alternative to the biceps curl)

You will need:

- 1 Mah Jongg set
- 1 Mah Jongg card
- 1 oversized card table
- 1 monogrammed table cover
- 4 players

(Additional materials may include pictures of grandchildren, travel folders, recipes, house plans, and ice water [from the bottle, *not* the tap] with lemon.)

For this exercise, you must have a working knowledge of the game of Mah Jongg. For those of you who do not know a crak from a bam, Mah Jongg is an ancient Chinese pastime, the rules of which have been interpreted and perfected by mavens from the Catskills to the foothills.

Although some say the origins of Mah Jongg can be traced to the time of Confucius, we believe the game originated with our foremothers who, rumor has it, passed the time waiting for Moses to return from atop Mt. Sinai with the Ten Commandments by playing a few hands-but we digress.

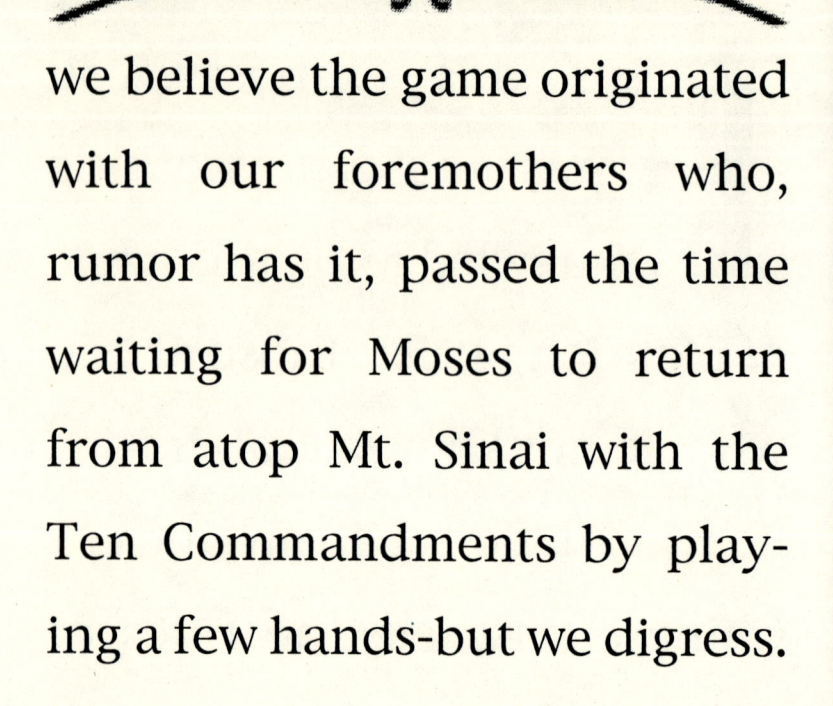

Now to the exercise:

Place the racks on the table in front of each player. After the tiles have been shuffled, build walls of tile, face down, in two layers in front of each rack. Make sure the racks are placed as far apart as possible, and as you begin the Charleston (the passing of unwanted tiles from player to player) build a steady rhythm.

1) Right, across, left.

2) Left, across, right.

Take your pulse — you're ready to begin the Mah Jongg stretch.

As you pick and discard tiles, extend your arm as far as possible. Do not bend your arm; feel the pull from shoulder to wrist.

Now, return to your original position while the other players have a turn. Continue until Mah Jongg is called and a player's exposed hand of tiles is declared valid. Repeat the exercise.

The amount of repetitions

depends upon the length of time per hand of Mah Jongg played, the duration of the game, and how much gossip is shared.

Appropriate times for this exercise may vary depending on each player's schedule, i.e., manicure/pedicure appointments, car-pools, massages, committee meetings, etc.

After a day at the table, you'll have worked on those

arms, burned a few calories, and maybe added a quarter or two in change to your bottom line.

Notes and Reminders:
- ✓ Get recipe for Susie's slimmed-down version of chocolate turtle delight using skim milk instead of cream cheese and baby prunes instead of oil
- ✓ Call Mildred to substitute next week
- ✓ Check ruling on Mah Jongg in error with National Mah Jongg League
- ✓ Get number of new carry-out restaurant in the neighborhood

Chapter II
The Worry Walk

(An aerobic original)

Yentas have been perfecting this exercise before anyone ever used the word "aerobics." Although best done in a state of high anxiety while awaiting a crisis real or imagined, the worry walk was never intended to increase your heart rate, but rather to keep it down.

Scenario:

Your husband/child/parent

is 30 minutes late for dinner and has not called although the line has not been busy, and the phone is in working order.

The weather bureau has issued a forecast for freezing rain, high winds, and low visibility. You hear sirens. Before hyperventilating, take your pulse and begin the worry walk.

This can be done room to room or window to window.

Continue until you see approaching headlights. Check to see the make of the car, and if it proves to be your loved one's, stop and slowly exhale. If it is not, then continue the exercise at an even pace.

Please remember to breathe, and if the walk lasts too long, get out of those three-inch heels!

Scenario # 2

The kitchen sink is stopped-up, you're having a dinner party, and you're waiting for the plumber. Take your pulse and start the worry walk.

Scenario #3

It's your day to do errands and you have a flat tire, and you're waiting for AAA. You were told someone would be there in 15 minutes. After that time has passed plus 15 minutes more, start the worry walk.

The worry walk is effective whenever you are awaiting the arrival of people, news, or decisions, indoors or outdoors, in corridors of hospitals, airports, and courtrooms. It can be done several times a day and is a good stress reliever and calf strengthener.

Notes and Reminders:

- ✓ Call podiatrist for appointment.
- ✓ Ask Lindy for the name of her chiropractor
- ✓ Take shoes to Quick Repair
- ✓ Have windows washed

Chapter III
The Jewelry Lift

This exercise can be done in the privacy of your own home if you have the equipment needed.

In order to perfect this particular form of strength training, jewelry in specified weights is required. For our novice yentas, 14 carat is the lightest weight acceptable for the exercise to be beneficial, thereby requiring you to wear several gold bracelets and chains at the same time. (If this is a problem, maybe you have a friend in the business, and you can try on a selection of the merchandise — hopefully on a regular basis.) Beads, pearls, and diamonds by the yard are alternatives.

For best results, a good gold watch with a wide band, two or three bracelets in precious metal, i.e. gold or silver--and a few rings of semi-precious or precious stones will enable you to achieve the proper weight and balance for each arm.

With jewelry fastened securely, raise your arms slowly so that your hands are eye-level, hold for a count of 10, take a deep breath, *kvell and relax. Only sterling and gold pieces give you the proper weight. Costume jewelry, gold-

---

* Kvell (Kvell), *Yiddish,* verb: to take pride in or receive pleasure from

filled or silver-plated, will never achieve the desired results.

When you have mastered this phase, you're in good shape and can move up to 18 carat for that extra metabolism boost, not to mention a heightened sense of well-being.

Notes and Reminders:
- ✓ Get telephone numbers of jeweler and appraiser
- ✓ Buy a new issue of Town and Country magazine
- ✓ Find a good jewelry repair person

Chapter IV
The Shopper's Pull

Required equipment:

- Comfortable shoes
- Large handbag now updated to the fanny pack
- Credit cards
- Cash
- Checkbook
- Mall directory
- Bifocals for reading sale prices
- Small bottle of water and a few peanut butter crackers if there's no time for lunch

You don't golf or play tennis, you haven't ridden a bike since grade school, you think gyms spread germs, and the only skiing you enjoy is apres--so how do you work up a sweat? You shop!!

The best area for this exercise is a mall, but a specialty shop will do. Luckily the shopper's pull can be done in your own home town or during any trip anywhere in the U.S. or abroad. No matter the venue the shopper's pull will bring out the athlete in you.

You know the routine. Park your car as far from the entrance as possible. Head for your favorite store. Find the racks with your size. (The size you are *now*--not the size you plan to be.)

Turn away any helpful

salesperson (an oxymoron if we ever heard one!). Pull the merchandise from the rack-lift it in front of you-drape it over your left arm-and repeat until you cannot hold any more clothing. (This is an excellent form of strength training).

Proceed to the nearest dressing room. Pull garments on, pull or push garments off. Repeat until you've tried on everything at least once, and for some articles, if you're undecided, try them again and again.

Take your pulse. Feel the endorphins elevating your mood. You know you've hit your peak when you find the perfect designer dress at 75% off.

If you have the stamina, you can try another store, and repeat the exercise. If not, there's always tomorrow.

Notes and Reminders:

- ✓ Call for alteration appointment.
- ✓ Sign-up for Weight Watchers.
- ✓ Call Goodwill.
- ✓ Check out new lipstick shades.

Chapter V
The Beach Bends

(So who needs yoga?)

You will need:
- 1 swim suit preferably black and with tummy control
- Sunscreen
- Something for the head a *shmata or straw hat

This is a very gentle, soothing motion.

---

* Shmata (Shmata), *Yiddish*, noun: a rag

Sorry, but this is not water aerobics, and the exercise must be done where there's sand and waves. We believe it originated in Miami Beach in the 50s by some over-fifties who had just been to the hairdresser.

The Routine:

Wade far enough into the ocean so that the water comes to your knees or thighs. Bend to a crouching position. You are one with the sand and the sea.

Take a deep breath. Look straight ahead and watch for the waves. As one approaches, raise high on tiptoes while raising your arms. As the wave passes, exhale and resume the crouch position.

Repeat until it's time for lunch, more sunscreen, or the tide goes out. (You can crouch a little deeper and raise a little higher if you have a grandchild holding each hand.)

Notes and Reminders:
- ✓ Call the tanning salon
- ✓ Get a hairdresser appointment
- ✓ Order cellulite cream
- ✓ Call travel-agent
- ✓ Shop for bathing suit cover-up

Chapter VI
The Bean and Barley Upper Arm Reducer

You can tell us the truth. Your sleeveless blouses and dresses are stuffed in the back of the closet, or you've given them all away. It's those arms.

You can't bear to look at them, so you know no one else can. You can't find your free weights, and you don't have time for liposuction. Do not despair, help is as close as your pantry.

Find your favorite bean and barley soup recipe. *Double* the amount of barley you usually use. As the soup begins to thicken, start stirring.

Keep stirring until you feel the burn in your upper arm. When the right arm tires change to the left. Switch back and forth until the soup is done. You'll probably have to add a little water or stock before serving, but in addition to upper arm exercise, you'll now have a freezer filled with soup for that unexpected company.

If you have no beans and barley in your pantry, split peas will work just as well.

Notes and Reminders:

- ✓ Clean out pantry
- ✓ Clean out freezer
- ✓ Ask Dorothy about liposuction
- ✓ Call Jenny Craig
- ✓ Check out plastic surgeons on the Internet

Chapter VII
Eavesdropper's Eye Strengthener and Jowl Firmer Isometrics

The following scenario has happened before and will happen again. Make the best of it. You're having lunch with a business associate in a popular restaurant.

Two of your closest friends are sitting at a table within hearing distance from you. In the middle of your business associate's conversation, you overhear your friends mention another friend's name.

You are dying to know what they are saying, but you do not want to be rude to your companion. This is a great exercise opportunity.

Without moving your head, open your eyes wide and keep them fixed on the pupils of the person with whom you are dining. Take a deep breath and slowly exhale.

With your lips together,

raise the corners of your mouth to smile slightly, simultaneously lifting and jutting out your chin. Hold. Breathe only through your nose. Continue staring at your companion while you listen to the gossip being shared by your friends at the next table.

Without exception, no matter what you have overheard, you may not turn, gasp, blush, chuckle, guffaw, or show any signs that you are aware of anything other than what your companion is saying.

Feel the tension. Keep breathing, hold your head steady, and do not blink. Occasionally utter an hmmm or umm huh so that a vocal reply is unnecessary and your hearing is not compromised.

When you've heard all you want, relax your gaze, lower your chin, and verbally answer any questions or make any expected comments. Repeat the exercise when you hear another name or incident of interest to you from your friends' table (or any other table for that matter).

In addition to strengthening the eye muscles and firming the jowls, your power of concentration and mental acuity should be enhanced, not to mention your being one of the first to know the latest news.

This exercise can be done at parties, beauty salons, or any spots where friends gather.

Notes and Reminders:
- ✓ Call Aesthetician
- ✓ Call Ophthalmologist
- ✓ Call Optometrist
- ✓ Check time for yoga classes
- ✓ Get more aspirin
- ✓ Call friends ASAP

Chapter VIII
The Cellular or Portable Phone Twist

(A neck strengthener)

You will need:

❖ 1 cellular phone or one cordless phone

This can be done in the car, the supermarket, at home, at the beach, on an airplane, in the garden, while walking the dog, or waiting in any line.

In order to get the full benefit of this exercise you must not use your hands to hold the phone. Instead, after placing the call or when you answer, place the receiver atop your shoulder and cradle it in the crook of your neck.

Make sure the instrument fits snugly and the mouthpiece and earpiece are in the proper place for hearing and speaking. Your hands are now free to finish any task you were doing when the phone rang, thus enabling you to spend more time on this routine, unless the caller is boring, and you need an excuse to hang up.

Feel the pull of the neck muscles as you hold the phone in place. Change sides every few minutes to avoid cramping. (The only time your hands should touch the phone is to answer call waiting.)

When you change sides, pause when your head is upright for a count of ten, before placing the phone on the opposite shoulder. Breathing should remain steady and calm, no matter the conversation or the caller.

If the call is not altogether pleasant, and feelings of hostility, anger, anxiety, or guilt are being generated--do yourself a favor and hang up. You can always try the routine the next time the phone rings. Solicitation calls are never a part of this exercise program.

Some tasks that could be completed while talking are flower arranging, retrieving e-mail, knitting, rolling out a pie crust, cleaning out the refrigerator, making a to-do list, putting on panty hose, basting a chicken, folding laundry, changing a grandchild's diaper, sending a fax, sewing on a button, going through the mail, touching up your nails, etc.

Notes and Reminders:
- ✓ Call orthopedist
- ✓ Call masseuse
- ✓ Get caller I.D.
- ✓ Check into a day spa
- ✓ Check price of a phone headset

Chapter IX
Challah or Pumpernickel Knead

(For the hands and fingers)

Unfortunately, with the manufacture of bread machines, the springing up of neighborhood bread bakeries, and the advent of acrylic nails, this exercise has become obsolete. Touch-tone dialing on your cellular could be a substitute, if you do not use speed dialing.

Notes and Reminders:
- ✓ Find out if challah's on Sugar Busters
- ✓ Call for manicure appointment

Chapter X
Watch the Grandchildren Stairclimber and Complete Workout

Whatever your grandchildren call you--granny, nana, mimi, bubie, grandma--at the end of this exercise you can be called "fit."

Watching the grandchildren is a misnomer, for you are never still while they are in your care. Conditioning begins when your first grandchild is born.

Make sure you add a good

pair of tennis shoes for yourself when the baby's layette is bought.

Scenario:

Your daughter (a yenta-in-training) calls and asks if you are free to watch her one-year-old son who crawls and has just started walking. You tell her you would be delighted, because you are waiting for a repairman who should have arrived by 10.

Since it is now 12 noon, he should certainly be on the way-so you have to be home anyway. Your daughter tells you that your grandchild will probably nap, since he has not slept that morning.

They arrive-the repairman is still on the way-and you notice how wide-awake the child is. Your daughter says goodbye after filling you in on the dos and don'ts (like you *never* raised a child yourself!) and tells you she'll return in a few hours.

Take your pulse-you're ready to begin.

After numerous attempts to put the child to sleep by laying him in the crib and lifting him out when he starts to cry, you give up and put him down on the rug.

Your precious grandchild

starts to crawl and discovers the steps to the second floor. He knows how to go up but not down.

He climbs up two steps-you climb behind him, lift him, and bring him down. He laughs and starts to climb again-up three steps.

You climb behind him, lift and bring him down once more. He continues climbing. You continue behind him, lifting, and walking down until he is ready for a snack and you are ready for the nap he will never take. Repeat until your daughter returns or the repairman arrives.

Other scenarios:

The same child is now four years old. He no longer naps. Your yenta - in - training daughter calls again. You have a new repairman-the previous one never came or called-and as luck would have it, he's due to arrive any moment, so yes you will be at home and would be happy to "watch" your grandson.

It's a lovely, spring day, and your grandson wants to climb the jungle gym in the back yard.

He can climb up but cannot get down.

He climbs one rung you lift

him down.

He climbs two, you climb one and lift him down.

He climbs three, you climb two and lift him down.

You pray for rain. Repeat until your grandchild finds something else to climb, your daughter returns, or the new repairman arrives.

As your grandchildren grow and as more are added to the family, you will use muscles you never knew you had and play games you remember from your own childhood when backs were limber and legs were nimble and quick.

Strength-training equipment, weights, treadmills, and rowing machines could never condition you like the activities you engage in with your grandchildren.

In the course of a single session, you will bend and

stretch, lift and carry, squat and crawl, climb, walk, run, kick, jump, twist, stoop, throw, push, pull, skip, hop, laugh, and cry. (Iron women triathletes have nothing on you, for as your grandchild matures, you will bike, run, swim, play basketball, baseball, golf, hop-scotch, tennis, jump rope, water and snow ski, even if you never have before and do not know how to now).

We highly recommend this form of exercise. And although we may complain of soreness, tiredness, and aggravation, this complete body workout is a pleasure for any yenta. Breathing, however, is very important. Remember to breathe in through the nose and out through the mouth, or you may stop breathing altogether.

Notes and Reminders:

- ✓ Call Canyon Ranch
- ✓ Book a cruise
- ✓ Cancel personal trainer
- ✓ Buy linament

Have at the ready:

- ✓ Baby-sitter's number
- ✓ House-cleaner's number
- ✓ Baby-sitter's number
- ✓ Carpet-cleaner's number
- ✓ Baby-sitter's number

Chapter XI
When Calories Don't Count and other *Bubameicies

---

* Bubameicie (Bu-bu'-mice-a), *Yiddish,* noun: made-up story, an old wive's tale.

Yentas like to eat.

We like to eat at life-cycle events (weddings, bar-mitzvahs, anniversary celebrations).

We like to eat on holidays, even the minor ones.

We like to eat on vacations (especially cruises) and homecomings. Yentas turn to food not only as recreation but as salvation. We eat when we're nervous, when we're depressed, when we're anxious, and when we're stressed.

In other words, food is at the core of every card-carrying yenta, but there are times when, contrary to all information, we know that the substance of the act does not necessitate counting calories.

The following is a short list of such instances to keep in mind.

Calories do not count:
1. Before, during, and after sex
2. When the carton of ice-cream stays in the freezer, and you walk back and forth from the couch for a spoonful or two or three
3. When no one is watching
4. After a dentist appointment and your

mouth is numb
5. When you finish what's left on your husband's plate before the dish goes in the dishwasher
6. When you're trying to get your grandchild to eat, and you taste a few bites to show how good the food is
7. When you sample the grocery store giveaway
8. While you're cooking

9. Preceding or immediately following exercise
10. When you don't like what you've eaten
11. If you have a virus
12. When you eat on an airplane (if you're still having dinner when you land)
13. If the food is raw
14. On vacation

Chapter XII
Calorie Count of Favorite Snacks

(valuations are for the *One Bite* you take from someone else's serving)

To determine your calorie count, you must first count the number of bites you take to finish one serving, then divide that number into the calories per serving stated on the carton or package. Otherwise, just wing it.

* Ben and Jerry's (any flavor)
* Haagen Daz (any flavor)
* Low Fat Yogurt (any flavor)
* Frozen Snickers or Milky Way

* Guacamole
* Chips
* Movie popcorn
* Brownies
* Chocolate cake
* Cheese cake
* Rugulah
* Streudel
* Biscotti
* Pecan pie
* Key-lime pie
* Krispy Creme donuts
* Reuben sandwich

- Club sandwich with extra mayo
- Steak-cut french fries
- Enchiladas
- Three-cheese lasagna
- Quesadillas
- Spaghetti with meat sauce
- Pasta with pesto
- Egg Salad on whole wheat
- Chicken salad on whole wheat with Thousand Island on the side
- Hot pastrami sandwich

* Nova and cream cheese on a bagel
* Bread pudding with sauce
* Bread pudding without sauce
* French toast

Chapter XIII
A Yenta's Favorite Names and Numbers

* Trainer/Gym
* Favorite restaurant
* Favorite take-out
* Maseusse
* Hairdresser
* Manicurist
* Travel agent
* Chiropractor/Orthopedist
* Make-up specialist
* Housekeeper

* Housekeeper's daughter
* Daughter
* Daughter-in-law
* Daughter-in-law's parents/Son-in-law's parents
* Lawyer
* Private detective
* Best friend
* Therapist
* Rabbi or Minister
* Pro-shop
* Decorator

* Nutritionist
* Day-spa
* Jeweler
* Caterer
* Party planner
* Stockbroker
* Ex-husband
* Personal shopper
* Bank
* Florist
* Alterations lady
* Alterations lady's translator

* Realtor
* Psychic/Astrologer
* Aromatherapist
* Electrician
* Plumber
* Painter

Chapter XIV
Blank Pages

Use these for a personal journal, a to-do list, addresses, a food diary, measurements, important dates, shopping needs, recipes, your horoscope, or a thought for the day.

Epilogue

This book highlights creative exercise routines. However, you may have some ideas on broadening or expanding the regimen. If so, we'd love to hear from you. Who knows, the yenta's guide to exercise sequel could be forthcoming.

We plan to keep our minds and bodies busy and hope you

do the same. Please pass this book on to your friends or better yet, let them buy their own. Keep this for a handy reference, and as part of the watch the grandchildren complete workout routine, let your charges color the pictures while you take a deep breath.

About the authors:

Raye Ann Greenbaum, an art broker, wife, mother and grandmother, and Jackie Tepper, a wedding consultant, wife, mother and grandmother, became yentas without even knowing it. Midlife came with no crisis for either, but with the realization that the college diplomas they had once carried under their arms had been replaced with sagging skin. Tired of the daily barrage of "how to," "why to," and "when to" exercise programs and diet books, they decided to take a comical approach to achieving fitness by creating imaginative routines that could be integrated into a busy social schedule without compromising the lifestyle women of a certain age enjoy.

About the Illustrator:

Betsy Hoffman is a professional artist, wife, mother, and yenta-in-training.